From Group-Work to Teamwork:

How to Turn a Group Experience into a Great Experience

Shannon Graves
Richard Hoefer

The Center for Advocacy, Nonprofit and Donor Organizations (CAN-DO)
University of Texas at Arlington School of Social Work
211 S. Cooper Street • PO Box 19129 Arlington, TX 76019

Find us online at www.uta.edu/can-do

From Group-Work to Teamwork

This document is authored by and is the copyrighted material of Richard Hoefer and Shannon Graves.

© 2014 Richard Hoefer and Shannon Graves

Usage Guidelines
You do not have permission to copy, redistribute, or republish this work without the express written consent of the authors.

Find us online at www.uta.edu/can-do to access a constantly growing library of resources for nonprofit advocacy and human services management.

Table of Contents

Introduction: About this Report..4
Part I: Assessing Your Group.. 6
    Group Dynamics 101: Know Your Team...7
    Common Group Challenges..13
Part II: Five Steps to Tightening Your Team...18
    Step 1: Use Groups (And People) Wisely 19
    Step 2: Structure for Success 22
    Step 3: Spark Participation 24
    Step 4: Create Meaningful Dialogue 27
    Step 5: Allow Healthy Conflict 30
Wrap-Up and Summary...33
Additional Written Resources...34
Free Video Resources from CAN-DO...36
Can We Do Something More for You?...37

Introduction: About this Report

Despite our different interests, personalities, and career goals, we all want similar things in our work environment. We want to feel that our work is important and that it is making a difference. We want to feel supported, respected, and trusted. We want to be acknowledged for our contributions. Increasingly however, our efforts in the workplace rely on our successful engagement with others to meet these needs.

The use of groups and teams in the American workplace is growing, and effective teamwork has been associated with major performance gains and increased innovation. Alongside the stories of successful teams, however, is another less popular story. Teamwork is hard. Teamwork is complex because it requires team members to manage multiple relationships while efficiently dividing and coordinating tasks. When relationships or team processes break down, group-work can easily harm organizations more than they help.

The good news is that the popularity of team work has inspired a plethora of research into forming more effective groups and teams. As a result, we now know more than ever about avoiding the pitfalls of poorly planned teamwork. We also have access to an array of innovative solutions which have been proven to increase the power of our teams in the workplace.

The goal of this short report is to simplify and summarize the most important principals of using teams in the workplace. It provides a brief overview of the factors that affect team performance and the most common challenges that groups face when they come together. Most importantly, the largest section of this report focuses on practical solutions – news you can use – for turning your work group into a coordinated, communicative, successful team.

How to Use This Report

This report is organized into two parts. Part I is designed to guide you in *assessing your group* and identifying the challenges which are most affecting your performance. Part II provides practical suggestions for *tightening your team*. Not all of the problems or solutions may apply to your team, so carefully assessing your needs will help you focus your attention on the most relevant sections.

It is also likely that factors you are currently unaware of may be influencing your team outcomes. For that reason, we recommend reading this entire short report before finalizing your diagnosis and moving on to troubleshooting. Finally, remember that this report is a summarized and simplified version of a much larger body of research that can help further inform you work with groups and teams. If you are ready for next steps or more targeted recommendations, we encourage you to contact the Center for Advocacy, Nonprofit and Donor Organizations using the information in the final pages of this report.

Part I:
Assessing Your Group

Group Dynamics 101: Know Your Team

Group dynamics can be described as all of the variables in play when a group of people comes together which affect the outcome of their interactions. A dynamic is not a bad thing or a good thing – just a characteristic of the group, its members, or its larger environment. The dynamics of a group are, well, dynamic. In other words, they *cause* something. In this case, they cause your team to succeed, to fail, or to hover in the middle in a place called "mediocrity." Let's review some of the dynamics that are most likely to affect group work. As you read each section, take a few moments to write down the key dynamics of your members, your team, and your environment that are affecting your group performance.

Assess Your Members

Groups are made up of people. The knowledge, skills, and abilities of your individual group members are important dynamics that affect performance. Consider the questions on the following page and take the time to write down thoughtful responses that acknowledge each member of your team. As you do so, remember that strengths and weaknesses refer not only to workplace skills but also to personality and character traits. In some cases, the same quality could be a strength *and* a weakness.

Assessment Question 1: What are your team members' strengths and weaknesses? (List each member by name)

_____
_____
_____
_____
_____
_____

Assessment Question 2: What are your (the leader's) strengths and weaknesses?

_____
_____
_____
_____

Assessment Question 3: What are the training needs of individuals/team?

_____
_____
_____
_____

Assess Your Team

In addition to the traits of group members, the traits of your team matter. The size, structure, patterns of interaction, and cohesiveness of your group are all dynamics that affect the way you will coordinate and communicate. Consider the following factors in light of your team.

Assessment Question 4: Groups take time to form, acclimate to each other, and establish common values and norms. Describe your group's stage of development.

_____

_____

_____

_____

Assessment Question 5: How many relationships are involved and are there any relationships that have special dynamics? (e.g. one member is another member's best friend, worst enemy, parent, or direct supervisor)

_____

_____

_____

_____

Assessment Question 6: What communication styles are used?

_____
_____
_____
_____

Assessment Question 7: How often does conflict occur and how is it handled?

_____
_____
_____
_____

Assessment Question 8: What are the written rules and the unspoken norms of your group? Are they similar or different?

_____
_____
_____
_____

Assess Your Environment

It's important to remember that your group does not operate in a bubble. The nature of your task, the sense of urgency or stress present, and the way group members are selected, monitored, and rewarded all affect the way the team will interact and perform. Consider the following elements of your group environment.

Assessment Question 9: What is your task, and how complex is it?

_____
_____
_____
_____
_____
_____

Assessment Question 10: How suitable does the task appear to be for group work? (Can the responsibilities easily be shared?)

_____
_____
_____
_____
_____

Assessment Question 11: Which features of your work environment support or challenge the group's progress?

Assessment Question 12: Is there a mechanism for progress to be monitored and rewarded? Does it reward individuals or the group as a whole?

Common Group Challenges: The Big Three

Now that you are familiar with some of the dynamics that may be influencing your team, let's explore some common challenges that groups experience as a result of unmanaged dynamics. In our work with groups in nonprofit and academic settings, the "big three" challenges below are the most often experienced and the most highly detrimental to team performance. Rate your group after each subsection and evaluate your strength in each of these areas.

Social Loafing

In our work with groups in nonprofit and academic settings, the number one concern is that a few people do all of the work while others do little or none. Sound familiar? Indeed, research shows that when we form groups, the level of individual effort is reduced. This phenomenon is known as "social loafing" and results in one, two, or a few of the most motivated members doing more than their share of the work while other members become disengaged. When social loafing occurs, groups are actually *less* productive than the same number of individuals. Yikes! Rate your group on the following page in order to assess your group's participation levels. Average your scores so that you can compare your overall proficiency in this area to the other common challenges ahead. The higher your scores, the closer you are to the best practices for groups and teams.

Assessment Tool 1	**Strongly Disagree**				**Strongly Agree**
All members attend at least 80% of scheduled meetings and events.	1☐	2☐	3☐	4☐	5☐
All members contribute something every time we meet.	1☐	2☐	3☐	4☐	5☐
Effort is equally divided between all group members.	1☐	2☐	3☐	4☐	5☐
Our group accomplishes more together than we would individually.	1☐	2☐	3☐	4☐	5☐
Total all lines and divide by four.				=	_____

Luckily, groups can be structured and facilitated so that the social nature of working together increases rather than decreases effort. We'll talk more about how to ***structure for success*** and ***spark participation*** later.

Coordination Loss

Even when everyone actively participates, groups can struggle to coordinate their efforts in an efficient way. Have you ever participated in a vibrant brainstorming session, only to leave the meeting without a clear decision or direction? This is one sign that while you have engaged members, they still are not quite sure how to turn their efforts into clear plans and, ultimately, achieve successful outcomes. The more people in your group, the more challenging coordinating your efforts will be.

Assessment Tool 2	Strongly Disagree Strongly Agree
All members can clearly state the goals and objectives of the group.	1☐ 2☐ 3☐ 4☐ 5☐
Our group has a clear process for making decisions.	1☐ 2☐ 3☐ 4☐ 5☐
Every group member has a specific, tangible role in completing the task.	1☐ 2☐ 3☐ 4☐ 5☐
In our group, ideas are translated into action.	1☐ 2☐ 3☐ 4☐ 5☐
Our final results reflect the product of everyone's efforts.	1☐ 2☐ 3☐ 4☐ 5☐
Our group would agree that we are "on the same page."	1☐ 2☐ 3☐ 4☐ 5☐
Total all lines and divide by six.	= _____

Average your results for this section and compare them to those for Social Loafing. Is this an area of need for your team? Later, we'll address some ways to increase coordination by ***using groups wisely, structuring for success,*** and ***creating meaningful dialogue.***

Symbolic Participation

The third major challenge for high functioning teams affects even groups with lots of participation and excellent coordination of efforts. Symbolic participation occurs when participation is not meaningful, either because people who are participating don't actually have the knowledge and skills to make informed contributions or because their contributions are only socially motivated. When group members verbally support a decision that they don't actually think is best, or when group leaders ask for input that they don't intend to use just to make people feel good, the resulting participation is not real. Because symbolic participation fails to take advantage of the collective wisdom of the team, it is incapable of producing team outcomes which are better than individual efforts. People participate symbolically in order to avoid conflict, confrontation, or power struggles, but the real result is that team members feel undervalued and unheard.

Assessment Tool 3	Strongly Disagree				Strongly Agree
Our group members bring a diversity of knowledge to the table.	1 ☐	2 ☐	3 ☐	4 ☐	5 ☐
Our group members are not always of the same opinion.	1 ☐	2 ☐	3 ☐	4 ☐	5 ☐
When our group comes to a decision, it represents all of us.	1 ☐	2 ☐	3 ☐	4 ☐	5 ☐
When someone in our group disagrees, he or she speaks up.	1 ☐	2 ☐	3 ☐	4 ☐	5 ☐
Our group leader is willing confront *and* be confronted.	1 ☐	2 ☐	3 ☐	4 ☐	5 ☐
Members do not fear consequences if they go against the group.	1 ☐	2 ☐	3 ☐	4 ☐	5 ☐
Total all lines and divide by six.				=	_____

Again, compare your average against those on the previous scales. Is this a critical area for your team? Powerful participation can be facilitated when we *create meaningful dialogue* and *allow healthy conflict* – but more about that later!

What's Your Major Malfunction?

Review the scores for all three of common "malfunctions" that happen in groups. Do one or more sections stand out as needing attention? Does a particular line reveal an opportunity to improve your group performance with a targeted solution? If so, great! If the overall experience of your team has been less than what you desire, then finding a weakness in your team functioning is a good thing – a roadmap to brighter days! As you learn about the *Five Steps for Tightening Your Team* in the following pages, pay special attention to those solutions indicated at the end of your biggest challenge, as determined using Assessment Tools 1-3 in the previous few pages. Use the rating scales often to assess your movement toward your goal of becoming of a top-functioning team.

If you rated your group highly on all of the scales above, but still feel dissatisfied with your team outcomes, consider whether there may be something you are missing. Especially if you are the leader of the group, ask your group members to complete the scale too, anonymously, and compare their ratings to your own. Only through an open commitment to identifying challenges can you move your group to a high performing team.

Part II:
Five Steps to Tightening Your Team

Step 1: Use Groups (And People) Wisely

Have you ever participated in a team meeting or group project where you thought, "Do we really *all* need to be here for this?" The truth is that sometimes the answer is a resounding "No!" While working in groups can indeed lead to significant performance gains, this is not the case for every type of task. For some tasks, individuals are better suited and more efficient in delivering a return. The very first way that you can ensure a high functioning team is to be certain that you are making wise use of groups.

A good general guideline is that groups are most effective when the goal of the task is to produce a high volume of ideas or information, when the task requires diverse knowledge and skill sets, and when the task is easily divided into smaller parts. Groups may be less effective when the task requires a high quality product in a specialized area and when the task cannot be easily divided. See below for some common examples of tasks that are best completed by groups versus individuals.

Tasks Suited for Groups	Tasks Suited for 1 to 2
• Brainstorming • Collecting Data • Compiling Information • Compounding Expertise • Choosing Among Alternatives • Executing a Multi-Part Event	• Writing a Report • Developing a Complex Recommendation • Executing a Complex, Highly Specialized, or Single-Part Task

A Note about Efficiency: This section primarily addresses whether tasks are *efficient* and produce high quality results in groups. It's important to acknowledge that the goal of group-work is not always efficiency or even quality. Teamwork is also used when the goal is inclusiveness or fairness. An agency decision that requires strong buy-in by all staff may be well served to engage in a group process around the decision – not because the decision will be faster or better, but because everyone will feel involved in the outcome. The United States Congress is an excellent example of a group that is generally regarded as inefficient and imperfect. However, because in this case democratic representation is valued over efficiency, Congress is a better option than many alternatives.

Unfortunately, there is no exact science for determining the right way to approach a task. Be observant and flexible. Is the group making progress toward the task? Does it seem like the group is taking longer than necessary to complete tasks that don't require everyone's input? Would group members feel comfortable handing the project off to a capable individual, and does such an individual exist? If the answers to these questions are yes, take a moment to closely consider using the group.

Using People Wisely

We often hear the adage about getting right people on the bus, and the people in the right seats. You must not only be strategic about when to use groups, but you must also carefully decide who will serve on a group and what role each member will play. A wisely chosen group will allow each member to have a specific role which highlights his or her strengths and areas of expertise. Not all members may be required for all tasks, or members may serve different roles at different parts of the process.

Consider a relay race team. Runners partnering in a relay race have equal parts in the labor. However, they don't all have work to do at the same time. While one person carries his or her load, the rest of team rests or waits to pick up the next leg of the race. Runners are assigned to start or end the race depending on their strengths. Who can give the team the best lead? Who is most able to make up any lost ground in the final leg? By using the unique strengths of each runner wisely, the team runs the race faster and more efficiently than any one runner.

Refer back to Part I, where you listed the strengths and weakness of each of your team members. Are your members being used wisely? In the lines below, list any strengths that aren't being used fully.

_____

_____

_____

Now, list any team member weaknesses that are slowing down the group's progress. Is there a way to reallocate responsibilities so that all members serve in their areas of strength?

_____

_____

_____

Step 2: Structure for Success

When group members don't participate meaningfully, we often think, "They are so lazy" or "Why don't they care?" We may even conclude, "I guess I have to do everything around here!" In reality, group members are more likely asking themselves, "Where are we going?" "What is my role?" and "Why am *I* here?"

As the leader, it is your job to facilitate a consensus on these topics and establish clarity about how people should participate and how the group will work together. One of the best ways to ensure that the group process moves forward smoothly is to set up an initial structure that supports success. Structures that help guide and support the group include the purpose of the group, the roles that members will play, and the processes that will be used for communication, interaction, and decision-making.

Coming to an agreement on these structures is an excellent way to use the initial meetings of the group. By engaging all members in a conversation about what should happen in order for the group to operate smoothly, you increase the likelihood that members will follow their own guidelines. Even if your group is already established, it's never too late to start a conversation about how the group should be arranged. In our experience, members appreciate the opportunity to give input and to use their time more effectively. The process of deciding upon group processes is a wonderful opportunity to work through challenges.

Task the group with writing bylaws that include the following:
- ❑ The purpose and goals of the group
- ❑ The duration of the group
- ❑ The requirements of responsible membership
- ❑ The roles required to complete the group's task(s)
- ❑ How often the group will meet
- ❑ How meetings will be conducted
- ❑ How decisions will be made
- ❑ Other rules agreed upon by the group
- ❑ How and when the bylaws will be reviewed and updated

Check Back Often

An important benefit of establishing a firm structure for the group early on is that you also create a touchstone that you or other team members can return to if and when the group deviates from the plan. When the group struggles to make a decision or members become confused about their roles, you have only to point out how the group is currently operating is different from the processes the whole team agreed upon. You can now engage the group in a discussion about whether the processes should be updated or whether the current course of action should be adjusted.

Step 3: Spark Participation

As we pointed out in Step 2, it's easy to blame group members for their lack of participation. However true leadership of a team goes beyond providing an assignment and expecting results. Inspired leaders actively facilitate meetings and group processes so that they are engaging, meaningful, and rewarding.

Engage the Group

Think about a group or team you have been a part of which was fun and engaging. What were the characteristics of the group leader? Most often, people report that effective group leaders really *care* about the project and the team. This care shows up in the form of careful preparation, passionate speech, and a commitment to seeing the team be successful.

Plan meetings ahead of time and build in opportunities for people to participate and be active. Provide an agenda a few days in advance so that group members have a chance to prepare for a meaningful discussion. Facilitate the meeting so that everyone will be called upon to contribute something. If your meeting consists mostly of sharing information, little participation will occur. If you allow large spaces of unmoderated group discussion, the more vocal members will naturally override the softer spoken ones. Provide specific opportunities for participants to engage with one another and be heard by introducing creative tools and techniques to facilitate brainstorming, group decision-making, and teamwork.

Check out these toolkits for facilitation inspiration!
- http://www.mindtools.com
- http://www.experientialtools.com/
- http://www.teampedia.net
- http://facilitatingagility.com/
- http://www.facilitate.com/support/facilitator-toolkit/
- http://www.uspto.gov/web/offices/com/oqm-old/Facilitation.pdf
- http://hrweb.berkeley.edu/files/attachments/Team-Building-Toolkit-KEYS.pdf
- http://www.utexas.edu/facilities/about/qapi/documents/TeamBuildingToolkit.pdf

Acknowledge Effort

People like to be acknowledged and recognized for their work. When you accomplish group objectives, it can be tempting to acknowledge the entire team for their success. However research shows that recognizing individuals is more important than recognizing the team as a whole. Start a practice of regularly acknowledging people for their contributions to the team. The more your team members feel that their individual efforts are noticed and appreciated, the more likely they will be to extend themselves on behalf of the group. Meaningful acknowledgements observe the following guidelines:

- **Timely:** In order to encourage future effort, acknowledge the current effort as soon as it occurs or as soon as you notice it.

- **Specific:** Include what the person did and how it affected you or the team. "Thanks for being so great!" isn't nearly as effective as "Your attention to detail was critical in making our report high quality."

- **Personal:** Deliver the acknowledgement in a personal manner. Face-to-face exchanges are most personal. A handwritten note is more personal than an email or text message.

- **Public:** Alternate personal acknowledgements with public ones. Make your acknowledgement in a team meeting, in front of the group member's supervisor or coworkers, or in a company newsletter.

Step 4: Create Meaningful Dialogue

Many of the problems that teams experience can be solved by more conscientious communication. Making a habit of clear communication will not only strengthen the way your team works together, but will also add clarity to processes and tasks undertaken by the group.

Get Feedback Friendly

Have you ever worked on a team in which it was obvious that certain behaviors, habits, or processes were holding back the team... *but you didn't say anything?* Perhaps multiple team members were aware of precisely what wasn't working and even discussed it at lunch or in the bathroom... *but no one said anything?* The habit of not speaking up is an easy one to fall into, but the truth is that withholding useful feedback is irresponsible to the team and makes it impossible to succeed at a high level.

Cultivate a feedback-friendly culture by making a habit of exchanging constructive feedback. After each meeting or task, spend time debriefing. What went well? What was less than ideal? Constructive feedback acknowledges mistakes in the past but focuses on the future. What new or changed actions could improve the team's performance next time? Remember that a feedback-friendly culture means that team members must not only commit to giving feedback that is honest but kind, and also to receiving feedback in an open and non-defensive manner.

Get Crystal Clear

Meaningful dialogue requires group members to say what they mean and mean what they say. In other words, get crystal clear with what needs to happen, and always follow through. When something needs to take place, make the request clear and specific. A clear request should include exactly what needs to happen as well as the time that it needs to happen by. Likewise, insist on clear and specific commitments in return. A clear commitment either confirms that the action can be done by the requested time or makes a negotiation on the details of the request. For example, "I can't send out that memo by Friday, but I can do it by Monday." When it unexpectedly becomes impossible to deliver on a commitment, speak up quickly and clearly to resolve any difficulties resulting from the unfulfilled commitment.

Practice Generous Listening

Having meaningful dialogue isn't all about talking! It means listening to one another... *really* listening. In their best selling book, The Collaborative Way, Fickett and Gore describe this principle as "listening generously." A generous listener is open-minded and genuinely interested in what the other person has to say. He or she actually anticipates that the other person will say something valuable and insightful. One way to test your active listening habits is to try having a conversation where you add nothing of your own. Simply listen, ask for more information, and hear everything your conversation partner is saying. If this is challenging for you, then you might be at risk of some unfortunate "stingy" listening habits, like interrupting, monopolizing the conversation, or inadvertently using the other person's speech as a time to plan what you'll say next.

Generous listening also means making sure that you truly understand the speaker. Because you value the speaker's contribution, you want to make sure you hear it just right! Begin a practice of reflecting: "What I hear you saying is ____. Is that right?" This simple habit can eliminate many misunderstandings before they start. It also lets others know that you are listening and interested in understanding their input. For more guidance on listening generously, visit www.collaborativeway.com .

If You're Wondering, Ask…

Finally, there is an adage that goes, "If you're wondering, ask!" When your group is experiencing challenges with coordination or meaningful participation, the simplest course of action is to ask: "Why?" Use dynamic communication to assess, explore, and solve the challenges your group is facing. What a great use for the collective wisdom of your team!

Step 5: Allow Healthy Conflict

Even if all of the other recommendations in this report are in place, your group will be unable to succeed as a high functioning team without conflict. Oftentimes, we think of conflict as a negative, confrontational, or angry force. However healthy conflict will naturally arise when people with different knowledge, skills, ideas, and opinions come together to forge a single outcome. The purpose of groups is to aggregate diverse contributions into a better solution – this is the very reason why teams outperform individuals on many tasks!

Teams must view conflict as an opportunity for innovation. When you dodge conflict to avoid feeling uncomfortable, you allow fear to stifle the group process. As the leader, it is your job to model and encourage the use of healthy conflict to form "full team" solutions that represent everyone's voice. Ask yourself the following self-assessment questions:

Self-assessment Question 1: As a leader and as a group member, how do you create/contribute to an environment that values vulnerability and accepts conflict?

_____

_____

_____

_____

Self-assessment Question 2: How often do you attempt to quickly block or resolve conflicts, or remove conflicts from the environment of the group?

_____

_____

_____

_____

Self-assessment Question 3: To what extent are you willing to demonstrate vulnerability by introducing high-risk or uncomfortable topics?

_____

_____

_____

_____

Building Trust

In order to engage in healthy conflict, group members must trust each other. Group members are able to engage in conflict constructively when they know that doing so will not damage their relationships with others in the group. By initiating, receiving, and resolving conflicts, you communicate to members that the group is a safe place to be creative, share authentically, and disagree.

Openly share with group members about the benefits of disagreeing, but recognize that actions speak louder than words. Model the value of conflict by welcoming the group to disagree with you, to suggest changes to the group process, and to address grievances with each other (and you). Avoid saying, "We'll talk about that later" unless the issue brought to light is truly a private or disruptive matter. Engaging in conflict will become easier over time, but will always remain uncomfortable. However, if you and your team members believe that your work is important and that a meaningful, collaborative outcome is important, then the reward of doing so is greater than the risk.

Wrap-up and Summary

Hopefully this report has started you on a journey of inspiring your team to work at a new level. Remember that many of the steps in this report won't cause changes to happen overnight. It may take trial and error to build a structure for success that meets the needs of your team members and your environment. It may take months or years to establish trusting ground for healthy conflict to occur regularly. However, if you stay tuned in to the dynamics, functions, and performance of your group and continue making adjustments, you will reap the benefits that meaningful teamwork has to offer to your workplace and the individuals within it.

Remember also that groups are as dynamic as the people who form them. As members come and go, struggle and grow, the dynamics of your group will continue to change. Use the assessment tools in Part I often, and be willing and ready to make changes to the structure and the practices of your team to reflect new people, new tasks, and the evolving context of your organization.

Additional Written Resources

If you've found the information in this report intriguing, be sure to look carefully at the next pages to find out more about CAN-DO and what some of CAN-DO's other information products are. Every book, report and video address one or more ways you can bring new ideas to your organization, improve skills, build knowledge and solve problems. You owe it to yourself to sign up at no cost on the email list to receive notifications on the latest products that will help you lead a better organization. Go to www.uta.edu/can-do to sign up now. When you do this, you'll gain access to a valuable exclusive report, available for free ONLY to CAN-DO subscribers.

This report is one in a series written by Dr. Rick Hoefer and Shannon Graves. They are available for Kindle e-readers and as print on demand soft-cover books. Below are links to Amazon.com to read about and order other reports that are currently available:

Old Organizations, New Tricks: Five Practical Keys for Unlocking a Learning Organization by Shannon Graves and Dr. Richard Hoefer. http://tinyurl.com/OldOrgNewTricks

Summary: This #1 bestselling social work book provides the right amount of information to assist your colleagues, your board, and your organization itself approach each day as an opportunity to get better, to improve, and to learn! This book, while short and easy to understand, will be your step-by-step companion on an exciting journey to becoming a learning organization.

Your Organization's Riveting Story: How to Write so that People Read, Remember and Respond by Dr. Richard Hoefer and Shannon Graves. http://tinyurl.com/YourOrgRivetingStory

Summary: Too many nonprofit, human services, and social work organizations have reports that are boring. This report will help you write an original, expressive, and downright riveting story about your organization. A riveting report will be read, remembered and responded to, with greater involvement and more donations.

Free Video Resources from CAN-DO

For timely CAN-DO tips and resources, subscribe to Dr. Hoefer's YouTube channel by searching for DrRickHoefer. You may also visit www.uta.edu/can-do for links to these highly ranked videos:

3 Ways to Raise More Funds Online:
https://www.youtube.com/watch?v=uwOBHV8JwLc

Decision-making Flow Chart:
https://www.youtube.com/watch?v=8ptq1SR0wok

Five Steps on How to Hire an Evaluator:
https://www.youtube.com/watch?v=hMEEBZJT4uE

How to Decrease Staff Turnover:
https://www.youtube.com/watch?v=GQqhsNsfWmc

How to Handle Nonprofit Mission Drift:
https://www.youtube.com/watch?v=m5Kwa8UnRIY

Leadership and Learning Organizations:
https://www.youtube.com/watch?v=fdojiqAb9Ss

Can We Do Something More for You?

CAN-DO! The Center for Advocacy, Nonprofit and Donor Organizations [CAN-DO] is the nonprofit research and capacity-building arm of the School of Social Work, University of Texas at Arlington. We are committed to working with nonprofits to help achieve higher levels of excellence and positive client outcomes.

We are self-supporting through developing mutually beneficial contracts with our nonprofit organizational clients. Initial consultations are always free and we work diligently to keep your investments in our services as low as possible.

For your free consultation, contact Dr. Rick Hoefer by email at rhoefer@uta.edu to begin a conversation about increasing the capacity and visibility of your organization. Dr. Hoefer is the Roy E. Dulak Professor for Community Practice Research at the School of Social Work at the University of Texas at Arlington. He directs the Center for Advocacy, Nonprofit and Donor Organizations (CAN-DO).

Dr. Hoefer specializes in translating cutting edge, best practice research into usable practice points for organizations. His passion is helping nonprofits succeed in providing high quality services to our communities. He has over 25 years of experience working in and with nonprofit organizations, assisting them in improving their services through program evaluation, advocacy, and management consulting. Dr. Hoefer has authored more than 30 published journal articles and 6 books and has given scores of presentations in the fields of nonprofit management, advocacy, program evaluation and policy practice.

Shannon Graves is a consultant with experience in nonprofit management, fund development, strategic planning, and community organizing. She specializes in bringing best practices to service systems and organizations through the effective and innovative development of policies, programs, and people.

www.ingramcontent.com/pod-product-compliance
Lightning Source LLC
Chambersburg PA
CBHW070723180526
45167CB00004B/1592